Elementary Morality

RAYMOND QUENEAU was born in Normandy in 1903 and studied at the Sorbonne before military service and a career working for the Gallimard publishing house. A novelist, philosopher, poet, mathematician and translator, he was a leading figure in twentieth-century French literary life, a prolific writer whose work touches on many of the major cultural movements of his time, from Surrealism to the experimental writing of the *nouveau roman*. In 1959 he published his best-known work, the novel *Zazie dans le métro*, which was a popular success both as a book and in the film adaptation by Louis Malle. In 1960 Queneau co-founded the 'Workshop for Potential Literature' or OuLiPo, a group of writers and scientists exploring the interactions between mathematics and literary forms. The group has included among its members Italo Calvino, Georges Perec and Harry Mathews, and still thrives today. Queneau died in 1976.

PHILIP TERRY was born in Belfast in 1962. He has taught at the universities of Caen, Plymouth and Essex, where he is currently Director of Creative Writing. His fiction, poetry and translations have been widely published in journals in Britain and America. His books include the celebrated anthology of short stories *Ovid Metamorphosed* (2000), *Fables of Aesop* (2006) and the poetry collection *Oulipoems* (2006).

DAVID BELLOS is Professor of French and Comparative Literature at Princeton University. A distinguished critic and translator, he is the author of the first biography of Georges Perec and Perec's foremost English translator. He has received many honours and prizes for his work, including the first Man Booker International Translator's Award in 2005.

RAYMOND QUENEAU

Elementary Morality
Morale élémentaire

Translated by
PHILIP TERRY

with an introduction by
DAVID BELLOS

CARCANET

First published in Great Britain in 2007 by
Carcanet Press Limited
Alliance House
Cross Street
Manchester M2 7AQ

A CIP catalogue record for this book is available from the British Library
ISBN 978 1 85754 948 5

The publisher acknowledges financial assistance from Arts Council England

Typeset by XL Publishing Services, Tiverton
Printed and bound in England by SRP Ltd, Exeter

Contents

Acknowledgements

I would like to extend warm thanks to Kevin Nolan for inviting me to read selections from this translation at the Cambridge Conference of Contemporary Poetry in 2006, and for subsequently publishing drafts of the first part in the CCCP Translation Series. I would also like to thank Tim Atkins for publishing a generous selection of the *quennets* in the online magazine *Onedit*. I would like too to thank friends and colleagues who helped with their invaluable support and advice, in particular David Bellos, Ann Davey, Clare Finburgh, Harry Mathews, Jean-Jacques Poucel, Stephen Rodefer, Marina Warner and, especially, for his expert comments on the final draft, Stuart McMenemy. Finally, I wish to thank Judith Willson and Michael Schmidt at Carcanet for their constant support and enthusiasm.

Introduction

Elementary Morality is the last book published by Raymond Queneau, and it seemed to its first readers to be quite different from all that had come before from the pen of France's most remarkable polymath. But Queneau never had been the kind of writer who did the same thing twice. This haunting and intricately crafted book of poetry shows not that Queneau was losing his grip as his health declined and his life wound inexorably down towards its end, but that the springs of invention remained as tight and powerful in the poet's old age as they had been in his youth and maturity.

Born in Le Havre in 1903, the son of a small shopkeeper, Queneau was a mathematician as well as a poet. He was drawn towards the Surrealist movement in the 1920s but broke with André Breton definitively after one of the many squabbles for which the group's leader was notorious. Queneau developed his own aesthetic principles in the 1930s, giving priority not to inspiration, the marvellous or the subconscious, but to order, craft and knowledge. He began publishing fiction in the same period, became an editor at Gallimard, and, after the Second World War, launched and directed the *Encyclopédie de la Pléiade*. Among his many unique achievements can be found a narrative of his own psychoanalysis in verse, a poetic dithyramb to the making of polystyrene, imitations of Renaissance poetry that turned into lyrics sung by Juliette Greco, a semi-pornographic journal of the Dublin uprising of 1916, contributions to combinatorial mathematics, a vast historical and biographical inquiry into literary eccentrics, and a campaign to win respect for the spoken language, whose phonetic, semantic and syntactic differences from school-book French were most memorably pointed out in an article showing the greater similarity between contemporary Parisian street-slang and the Native American language, Chinook, with which it has no connection whatsoever. His many novels reached only a limited audience until *Zazie dans le métro* – a sly, rambunctious and creative reinvention of Nabokov's *Lolita*, written in the *néo-français* dear to Queneau's heart – made his name a household word in 1959.

In 1960, together with his almost equally multiply-gifted friend François Le Lionnais (mathematician, chessmaster, conjuror, international civil servant, detective fiction collector, etc.), Queneau founded a research group devoted to the exploration of the potential interaction between mathematics and literature. This group, which is not a literary movement, and which still thrives today, was named Workshop for Potential Literature, Ouvroir de littérature potentielle, or OuLiPo for short. Bringing together outstanding members of the scientific community (Le Lionnais, Claude Berge, Paul Braffort, and now also Olivier Salon) with writers who have since acquired international reputations (Jacques Roubaud, Georges Perec, Harry Mathews, Italo Calvino), OuLiPo was Queneau's afterlife insurance policy, and *Elementary Morality* was his most profound and lasting bequest to it.

The volume consists of three distinct parts. The first was written rather slowly, in pieces, over a period of a year, between May 1973 and April 1974. Nineteen of these pieces were published in the *Nouvelle Revue Française* in January 1974.[1] The second and third parts were written rather fast, in barely more than six weeks, in April–May 1975. After a small amount of rearrangement to ensure that the totality comprised a numerically interesting quantity of 131 individual pieces (a prime number that is also a palindrome), Queneau published the volume in the autumn of 1975. A year later, he died.

The formal and thematic roots of *Elementary Morality* lie in what was for most of Queneau's life a hidden but unwavering interest in Eastern philosophy. In the note that he drafted to accompany the pre-publication of Part I in *Nouvelle Revue Française*, Queneau asks us to imagine the phrases of the 'noun' lines being punctuated by the sound of a gong, and

---

1   Some others appeared in the literary reviews *Bételgeuse* and *Confluent* a few weeks later.

to hear behind the shorter 'verb' lines a melody played on flute or reed-pipe – a sly but effective way of alerting us to the Chinese atmosphere of these formally unprecedented verses. The Chinese origin of the prose poems of Part III was however entirely secret until study of Queneau's manuscripts (in view of the posthumous publication of his *Complete Works*) revealed their presence, their extent and their intricacy.

The poems of Part I are in a regular but never previously imagined form. It did not arise from an intended act of invention, Queneau confided in his personal diary, but from the least Oulipian of all poetic sources – inspiration. 'Purely internal "reasons" determined this form', he wrote in the foreword to the poems' first publication. 'It did not derive from any prior mathematical or rhythmical exploration that can be made explicit.' However, in exploiting a form that seems to have come to him 'just like that', Queneau noted in his diary, 'I discover that I can use this new structure to "do Oulipo" (*faire de l'oulipisme*)'. The rules of the form are not hard to follow and can be represented thus:

> Three two-line stanzas, line 1 of each consisting of three phrases and line 2 of one phrase, each phrase formed by a noun–adjective pair
> *followed by*
> Seven lines of at least two and not more than seven syllables
> *followed by*
> One two-line stanza conforming to the same constraint as at the start.
>
> Rhymes, assonances, and repetitions between phrases and the 'middle lines' (what Queneau called 'the refrain') are not regulated but positively encouraged.

Queneau first titled the form *lipolepse* (from the Greek verbs for 'leaving out' and 'taking in'), but the OuLiPo immediately dubbed this new form the *quennet*, as it has one line more than a sonnet, and seemed to be, at least potentially, as easy to grasp, to copy, and to use as that most canonical of poetic forms. The form may have some relationship to the Chinese *liu-shi*, one of whose most elegant practitioners was none other than Li Po, whose name made him, quite fortuitously, a tutelary god of the OuLiPo.

All kinds of material can be used to construct an 'elementary morality' in the form of the *quennet*: phrases taken from a specified source (another poem, for example); autobiographical material; landscape, weather, memories – in fact, any of the material used to make poems of a more traditional kind. But not even Queneau can invent a new poetic form by an act of the will or the mind. The *quennet* may perhaps one day be seen as something as fertile and re-usable as the sonnet, but only time and poetic practice over the coming centuries will tell. At present, only Paul Fournel (Queneau's successor's successor as president of OuLiPo) has made extensive use of the form. Philip Terry's translation marks the first appearance of the *quennet* in English.

Parts II and III of *Elementary Morality* are prose poems: short paragraphs of dense, non-rhyming, non-regulated images, occasionally suggesting events or anecdotes, but principally evoking moods and states. In French, the prose poem arose in the nineteenth century, and its most celebrated pioneers were Aloysius Bertrand (*Gaspard de la nuit*, 1842) and Charles Baudelaire (*Petits poèmes en prose*, 1869). Widely used by Symbolist and Surrealist writers, the prose poem has also served as a vehicle of expression for modern poets like Francis Ponge and Jacques Réda. The prose poems of *Elementary Morality* III, however, have a source quite alien to the French tradition. They are meditations sparked off by the hexagrams of the oldest of the Chinese 'Books of Wisdom', the *I Ching*, commonly known as 'The Book of Changes'.

The text of the *I Ching* consists of divinations represented by a set of sixty-four abstract line arrangements called hexagrams. Each hexagram is a figure composed of six stacked horizontal lines, where each line is either *Yang* (an unbroken, or solid line), or *Yin* (broken, an open line with a gap in the centre). With six such lines stacked from bottom to top there are 2^6 (or 64) possible combinations. They are organised into eight classes, memorised as 'Heaven', 'Thunder', 'Water', 'Mountan', 'Earth', 'Wind', 'Flame' and 'Swamp'; each hexagram belongs to two classes (rather, is the intersection of two classes) and also has a mnemonic label,

Upper / Lower	Ch'ien Heaven	Chên Thunder	K'an Water	Kên Mountain	K'un Earth	Sun Wind	Li Flame	Tui Swamp
Ch'ien Heaven	1 Force	34 great invigorating	5 attending	26 great accumulating	11 pervading	9 small accumulating	14 great possessing	43 parting
Chên Thunder	25 without embracing	51 shake	3 sprouting	27 swallowing	24 returning	42 augmenting	21 gnawing bite	17 following suit
K'an Water	6 arguing	40 taking apart	29 gorge	4 enveloping	7 leading	59 dispersing	64 not yet fording	47 confining
Kên Mountain	33 retiring	62 small exceeding	39 limping	52 bound	15 humbling	53 infiltrating	56 sojourning	31 conjoining
K'un Earth	12 obstruction	16 providing for	8 grouping	23 stripping	2 field	20 viewing	35 prospering	45 clustering
Sun Wind	44 coupling	32 persevering	48 welling	18 corrupting	46 ascending	57 ground	50 holding	28 great exceeding
Li Flame	13 concording people	55 abounding	63 already fording	22 adorning	36 brightness hiding	37 dwelling people	30 radiance	49 skimming
Tui Swamp	10 treading	54 converting the maiden	60 articulating	41 diminishing	19 nearing	61 centre confirming	38 polarising	58 open

which is also its meaning. In the table on p. xi, only the meanings and the rank order are shown: the actual hexagrams and their realisation in Chinese writing do not seem relevant to understanding Queneau's poetry.

Dominos of ivory, wood (or plastic) marked with the hexagrams of the *I Ching* (and/or their mnemonics in Chinese or other characters) have long been used like tarot cards for fortune-telling, but the interest of the system – at least for Queneau – was its purported exhaustion of all possible circumstances by a combinatorium of simple figures composed of arrangements of the opposing and complementary forces of *yin* (suggesting 'order' 'more' 'masculine') and *yang* (suggesting 'disorder', 'less', 'feminine').[2] The *I Ching* appealed to Queneau's long-standing passion for exhaustiveness and for systematisation, and his ency-clopaedist's ambition to make all things fit together.

Queneau's interest in the *I Ching* was not new. In fact, it was when he was sorting out old cardboard boxes on 23 February 1974 – after the completion of the poems of Part I of *Elementary Morality* – that Queneau came across notes he had written in 1924 on Philastre's French transla-tion of the Chinese book of wisdom, and it is those notes, rather than the *I Ching* itself, that set off Queneau's composition of the sixty-four medi-tational poems that constitute *Elementary Morality* III. They were written in the order in which they are published, and it seems clear from at least some of them that the mnemonic associated with the number in the chart given above was the spring for Queneau's invention. Poem 48, for example, is located on the brim of a bottomless well, taking its cue from hexagram 48, the intersection of 'water' and 'wind', and known as 'welling'. Similarly, hexagram 36, conjoining 'earth' and 'flame' in the name 'brightness hiding', corresponds obliquely but not obscurely to the story of the athlete who misses the end of the race at the stadium by taking the wrong path, leaving spectators in the dark, watching an empty floodlit track (poem 36); and prose poem 46 treats hexagram 46, 'ascending', as a mystery of levitation. Readers may work out many

2   French Sinologists use a completely different transcription system for Chinese sounds and write *khièn* and *khouen*.

other correspondences, while remembering that Queneau neither numbered his poems nor published any indication of the role of the *I Ching* in their composition.

Almost equally hidden from the ordinary reader are the many oblique notations of Queneau's own life and work. He had first thought of publishing *Elementary Morality* under a pseudonym composed of his father's first name and his mother's maiden name, Augustin Mignot, and the presence of his mother in the first of the *lipolepses* as 'Dark Isis' (Isis being the Egyptian mother-goddess), and of his father as 'russet sun' in the second, sets the autobiographical sequence in motion. *Quennet 7*, with its 'foaming lighthouse, visible granite' and 'tough gorse' seems to evoke Normandy, Queneau's province of origin, which we find again in the place-names of *quennet* 13 ; number 15 alludes to the poet's youthful passion for boxing, and number 16's 'waterproof insomnia' may be as much a rumination on Surrealism as on dreaming. *Lipolepse* 20 evokes Queneau's military service in North Africa, and the 'razed town' of poem 23 is probably Le Havre, Queneau's place of birth, much of which was destroyed by Allied bombing in 1944.

The sense of the title eventually found for the collection, and now also used for the forms and devices it contains, is not easy to represent in English. *Morale élémentaire* suggests that the *elements* are involved – presumably, the sixty-four 'elements' that the table of the hexagrams of the *I Ching* generates – just as much as it suggests something *elementary* in the stripped-down form of the *lipolepse*. *Morale* suggests a code of behaviour as well as the moral of a story. Between a code of elemental truths and an elementary ethics, *Morale élémentaire* is both as ungraspable and as pregnant with meaning as the poems and prose texts it contains.

Permeating the poetic language of all three parts of *Elementary Morality* are several characteristically Quenellian interests. Mathematics, most obviously: spherical names, algebraic eagles in I.2, subtraction, division, exponential logarithms in I.3, children confronted with a mathematical problem in II.9, circles, squares and spheres in II.10, a polyhedron in III.10, integers, irrational and transcendent numbers in III.2, 'ten thousand things' (the original meaning of 'myriad', and also the alleged product of the table of hexagrams in the *I Ching*) in III.3, a Euclidian surface in III.31, 'juggling numbers all greater than zero' in III.34, integral calculus in III.53, a cube, a circle, spheres and astragals in III.58. Readers of Queneau's last novel, *The Blue Flowers*, may also recognise the ancient and medieval props that supply much of its comical and learned atmosphere: parapets, helmets, and Trojan wars in I.8, breastplate and blazon in I.39, warriors, pikes and cannon balls in II.13, a veritable lexicon of the Bayeux tapestry in II.14. The décor and themes of Queneau's earlier 'suburban' novels like *Loin de Reuil* and *Pierrot mon ami* – fairgrounds, clowns, ragpickers, vaudeville and puppet shows – also make frequent appearances in *Elementary Morality*: fortune-telling in I. 46, theatre in II.5, III.23, III.25, the *flâneur* or the ragpicker in II.7, the flea market in III.17, a fair in III.56, and the *banlieue* in III.61. Other perceptibly recurrent material evokes schooldays (I.24, III.15, III.16, perhaps III.58) and, as in so many of Queneau's poems and novels, the rain.

But these threads are woven together with innumerable other themes and interests, some clearly inspired by the mnemonics of the *I Ching* (swamp, thunder, mountain...), some alluding directly and indirectly to the matter of writing (typewriter, book, and scripts of various kinds), beneath an overarching intimation of the passing of time, and its imminent end, concluding with the 'eleven fifty nine, the end is approaching' of the sixty-fourth *kouà* of Part III, the one hundred and thirty-first poem of the collection. With its dense accumulation of rare words and names of rare things , *Elementary Morality* is also a collection of the treasures of the vocabulary. Where but in Queneau's poems will you find lexical treasures (with barely a liberty taken with the standard language, even by the translator) such as: argyric, borage, charfish, contractile, cretaudacious, cyproid, holoryhme, Kennedyas, Kimmeridgian cliff, ophidian, orthoptera, pododrome, pulverulent, quadratic reciprocity, sanious, scalene, soleabrious, solidungulate, subural, and ziggurat?

You mustn't
change barbaric

names
terms carried
on the backs of mules
on the backs of camels
rare words

No less clear than Queneau's defence of the lexicon is his assertion of the aesthetic and ethical principle that underlies all his work as a poet:

The law is tough, but it's the law; if you change it you may right an injustice, but you usher in disorder.

Reading and rereading these poems, in this crystalline translation of Philip Terry, what was obscure slowly becomes light, unseen connections bring coherence and greater depth, and yet the poetry remains, as Queneau always intended, simultaneously lucid and baffling. The last word is his:

Nothing but mysteries, you might well say. Nothing but mysteries.

David Bellos
Princeton NJ
18 May 2007

I

Dark Isis   Green fruit   Spotted animal
                     Clear neologisms
Red flower   Transparent attitude   Orange-coloured star
                     Clear springs
Brown forest   Russet boar   Bleating flock
                     Sparse tree

                     A boat
                     on the water
                     soleabrious
                     follows the current
                     A crocodile
                     bites the keel
                     in vain

Ochre Isis   Crumbly statue   Apricot totem
                     Clear neologisms

Russet sun   Russet moon   Blond stars
                      Spherical names
Blue flower   Strong metals   Lustrous horizon
                      Lyrical gestures
Cut grass   Immense swan   Flying sparrowhawk
                      Algebraic eagles

                      A sparrow
                      chirps
                      in the elm
                      A long song
                      unfolds
                      on the road
                      now

Brown sun   Green Venus   Heavy Sirius
                      Spherical names

Subtraction sum   Multiple division   Exponential root
                       Ordinary day
Drawn-out lime   Central pool   Extended pretext
                       Ordinary yesterday
Closed books   Open notebooks   Unreal calculations
                       Usual reflections

                       The sun that lasts
                       beyond midday
                       An obscure face
                       a vanished face
                       and some little
                       some little worries
                       on bright soil

Abstract sum   Multiplied union   Logarithmic increase
                       Ordinary day

Deaf hand	Dumb hand	Dense hand
	Expectant hand	
Tracer hand	Tracer hand	Tracer hand
	Drawing hand	
Fluid ink	Fluttering machines	Dazzled papers
	Writing hand	

Today's
ignorant
swans
protect
the silvery lake
from fires
and signs

Leaning ladder	Falling salt	Passing cat
	Protecting hand	

Grey children   Pure eagles   Singing quails
                                 Epicene things
Resounding organs   Unsteady loves   Trembling delicacies
                                 Scalene terms
Proper names   Transparent first-names   Illegitimate surnames
                                 Parallel lives

                                 Beneath the moss
                                 the woodlice
                                 coil up
                                 while
                                 beneath the elm
                                 grows
                                 spice

Singing organs   Resounding loves   Trembling quails
                                 Topical vowels

Crystalline flies	Plumed flashes	Buzzing clouds
	Critical words	
Spherical midges	Vague zigzags	Greying skies
	Epidemic words	
Gnawed trees	Crunching leaves	Naked branches
	Rustic words	

There is no more water
in the well
and the bucket
of bitter gout
is trickling away
in the river
at midnight

Displaced forests	Subdivided prairies	Uneven roads
	Critical words	

Wild wheat   Balas ruby   Tough gorse
                               Distant province
Unharmed viper   Transparent sapphire   Pink clover
                               Breast islands
Foaming lighthouse   Visible granite   Tough gorse
                               Distant province

                               The view of the horizon
                               remains impalpable
                               the roof of the houses
                               imputrescible
                               the oak all black
                               the priest in his chasuble
                               the wind without reason

Tough wheat   Polished ruby   Wild gorse
                               Incarnate clover

Protective parapets   Cursed crenelles   Encircling weapons
                             Agamemnon boiling
Singular combats   Plural enemies   Wartime tricks
                             Imprudent Nestor
Stolen captives   Blinded seers   Winged goddesses
                             Trojan wars

                             Achilles with his heel
                             his heart
                             full of wrath and bile
                             as the cauldron helmets
                             rallied on the plain
                             You could hear the snort
                             of a cardboard horse

Singular combats   Plural enemies   Wartime tricks
                             Immortal masterpiece

Drowsy marshes   Green swamps   Spewy bogs
         Latent waters
Dying flowers   Overripe fruit   Stagnant branches
         Drowsy marshes
Mauve bubbles   Secret ferments Racing fires
         Latent memories

         Passing
         the usual threshold
         the wood drifts
         beyond rot
         You must climb
         the slick
         greasy pole

Vermillioned wheels Glossy horses   Vertical arrows
         Village fête

Slow awakenings   Flat arousings   Premature wakefulness
                       Permitted nights
Exhausting sleepiness Latent snoozes   Murmured siestas
                       Indecisive days
Drowsy jobs   Halting action   Perished past
                       Grey habits

                       At the torrent's edge
                       the path zigzags
                       where is the happiness
                       of clear air
                       of the day blue
                       with the sun of yesteryear
                       where is the happiness

Exhausting sleepiness Slow awakenings   Passive days
                       Flickering memories

Old river-dweller Antique letters   Rare paraphs
        Eclipsed sun
Stacked sentences Full paragraphs   Thick chapters
        Mephitic moon
Browned books   Yellowed books   Cracked books
        Darkened sky

        You search
        a shelf
        for the trace of dust
        the bright silverfish
        the flaked-off leather
        the burnt-out crystal
        all you treasure

Browned books   Yellowed books   Cracked books
        Rising sun

Muddy sea   Uncertain river   Sanious water
                   Uncultivated streams
Filched stomachs   Squandered pennies   Sly needles
                   Exotic alcohols
Tasted gold   Swallowed silver   Absinthe pharmacies
                   Metallic potions

                   The thickness
                   of the fumes
                   the darkness
                   of the silhouettes
                   scarcely make
                   the weather vanes
                   budge

Silvery drinks   Golden binges   Alcoholic streams
                   Funerary pharmacies

Subtle goblets

Sautéed cards

Deceptive bouquets

Stale nutmeg
Diabolical tours
Stuffed dates
Pedagogical tours
Vivid trunks
Archaeological tours

Untangled hoops

Found digits

Mutant carafes

A barge
passes empty
passes quickly
downstream towards
Dieppedalle
Tancarville
or Radicatel

Gleaming posters

Inane automatons
Archaeological tours

Gnawed straps

Slow insomnia

Slow morning

Scattered ensemble

Real dream
Mortal friendship
Dreamt reality
Umbilical sun
Mediocre flowers
Contractile night

Here are roads
here are sounds
here are roads
here are towers
here are roads
heavy buildings
for the city

Slow morning

Midday rung

Clasped hands

Slow afternoon

Fading sun
Feeble night

Sterile dinner

Mechanical shock	Ovoid shot	Light balance
	Selenic vest	
Faded mirror	Mottled mirror	Rusted mirror
	Twisted face	
Columnist laughter	Enduring laughter	Scattered laughter
	Extinguished laughter	

The boxer
is in soap
he makes bubbles
he makes bubbles
The boxer
should give
us hope

| New mirror | Impromptu mirror | Unforseen mirror |
| | Extinguished laughter | |

Hollow dream	Pale dream	Pallid dreaming
	Empty clowning	
Hollow fantasy	Slow reverie	Cream fancy
	Running river	
Dense nightmare	Waterproof insomnia	Counting sheep
	Epidermic night	

If the cloud wished
to cover the whole sky
it was mistaken
Cruel despair:
the cloud dreaming
of covering the whole sky
with its pastel

Extinguished reverie	Sifted dream	Perforated sleep
	Epidermic night	

Full cloud   Roan cloud   Heavy cloud

Stretched earth

Heavy rain   Dense rain   Hard rain

Soaked sun

Falling water   Running water   Fallen water

Drenched moon

The fluvial road
out of breath
sings while running
its mouth full
It is very dark
under the rib
of the umbrella

Thick streams   Dancing streams   Banal brooks

Autumnal stars

Trotting dogs   Rolling boules   Running men
                         Impassive trees
Astray cyclists   Bouncing balls   Passing walkers
                         Visible trees
Morning round   September march   Started day
                         Imputrescible trees

                         Pine nuts
                         pine nuts
                         and a few papers
                         and a few fag ends
                         then a bit of grass
                         a bit of sun
                         and no stern eyes

Astray round   Impassive march   Busy day
                         Visible trees

Expected wait   Tense wait   Expired wait
                             Distant hour
Artificial rain   Prolonged rain   Constant rain
                             Impending rain
Half-open window   Ajar door   Whispering houses
                             Expected wait

                             A single cloud
                             covers the sky
                             and the sun
                             a single cloud
                             that smells of honey
                             and melts away
                             without a rainbow

Weary rain   Dreary rain   Dry rain
                             Distant rain

Tin soldiers	Lead soldiers	Wooden soldiers
	Trivial beings	
Wooden rifles	Lead axes	Tin lances
	Tiny weapons	
White rectangles	Black rectangles	Rubber-tipped arrows
	Secret tactic	

Stopping by the corn fields
sacks heavy with baguettes
we eat sausage–meat
cut into slices
It is hot. We drink wine
the lads call vinegar
We're waiting for the colonel

| Pasted posters | Well-informed posters | Imperious posters |
| | Comical war | |

Imprecise sun	Floating moon	Faded stars
	Identical day	
Tarred fumes	Cardboard clouds	Graffitied azure
	Identical night	
Whitish signs	Blueish traces	Faded letters
	Identical nature	

A caterpillar
on a reed
in the dark brook
Feet in the water
someone looking for charfish
holds out a reed
to the mini-beast

| Whitish sun | Blueish moon | Faded stars |
| | Divergent year | |

Violet violets   Iridescent irises   Rose roses
                   Banal flowers
Clever donkey   Subtle goose   Winged buzzard
                   Animal rapper
White gold   Red silver   Light bronze
                   Ornamental metals

Anyone
who runs in the sky
retracing the path of a comet
hears the muffled cry
of the hammer giver
of soaring
colourful sparks

White violets   Iridescent iris   Winged rose
                     Magic towers

Indecisive cliff   Grey hospital   Red lantern
Fluvial seagulls
Razed town   Plundered town   Crushed town
General ruins
Maritime birds   Observed flights   Diverse emigrants
Hibernal tints

Return to the country
small magic
the smell of absinthe
sometimes drifts by
in the dull streets
a heavy phantom
of grief

Observed flights   Émigré towns   Sequani flights
Hibernal tints

Alarming school	Soiled courtyard	Autumnal rains
	Dead leaves	
Purified notebooks	Exalted lexicons	Grave grammars
	White leaves	
Sunk sun	Fighting sun	Cloudless sun
	Long days	

At the year's end
Kings bring
exotic goods
At the other end
grow bushy
mathematical
declensions

New tar	Fallen leaves	Autumnal rains
	Started school	

Remaking monkey	Tinkering monkey	Recoating monkey
	Anthropoid monkey	
Imitative mime	Imaginary mime	Imagist mime
	Insipid Helot	
Restrained double	Confined double	Frustrated double
	Idiotic doppelgänger	

So who's afraid
It's the melancholy
hauler
He acts brave
but becomes grave
and monastic
in winter

Cleaned picture	Hammered pewter	Fringed felt
	Idiotic doppelgänger	

Running dog	Yelping dog	Fawning dog
	Domestic dog	
Running cat	Miaouing cat	Purring cat
	Domestic cat	
Running hare	Growling tiger	Orang-utan monkey
	Domestic dolphin	

At the zoo
the gawking visitor
looks at the
sluggish creatures
In the clear skies
a lone eagle flies
in the air

Running elephant	Croaking toad	Dancing bee
	Domestic fly	

Blustery vanity

Pot-bellied vanity

Suffocating stomachs

Coloured pride
Strangled violet
Suffocating pride
Crushed violet
Arrogant colours
Stripped violet

Malvaceous wheel

Foolish wheel

Obtuse pavanes

Paper boats
prowl the sea
A copper sun
floats in the air
A crescent moon
arrives later
wan

Muffled breezes

Murmured songs
Distraught violet

Whispering shadows

Gilded head   Silver arms   Copper stomach
                             Sideritic legs
Auric leader   Argyric breasts   Bronzed thighs
                             Metallic paws
Hollow sun   Empty moon   False stars
                             Comic comets

                             Once upon a time
                             two times
                             three times
                             wooden sabres
                             straw rifles
                             utopian armies
                             retailed

Pedestrian clay   Achilles heel   Spiked hoof
                             Ceramic pedestal

Chrysic cranium   Whitish shoulders   Cyproid paunch
                       Clay-like feet
Swollen brain   Overfull chest   Blocked intestine
                       Clay-like feet
Anaemic minutiae   Minuted exploits   Extorted minutes
                       Clay-like feet

                       Nobody is cooking
                       in the oven
                       Nebuchad rings
                       Ah what a misfortune
                       to dream only
                       of fragile
                       pottery

Cretaudacious tarsus   Cretaceous meta   Crushing ankle
                       Broken cuneiforms

Cold night   Frozen nocturne   Sleepless sleepover
                           Drawn-out dream
Windy draught   Rolled-up corridors   Half-open doors
                           Classified dreams
Harsh winter   Black winter   Hardy winter
                           Past vertigos

                           The clock turns
                           its back on spring
                           In winter the bell
                           rings in the sky of the dead
                           Midnight is about to ring
                           the hand tilting
                           towards the other spring

Whitewashed night   Transverse night   Vanquished night
                           Insane night

Winter wolf

Harsh trunks

Breaking waters

Bluish wolf
Distant song
Rustling bushes
Moonlit howling
Crunching road
Solitary cry

Severe wolf

Severe snow

Wintering countryside

For the children
little little
the pillow cries
with little shouts
For the children
a little older
the pillow lies

Winter wolf

Bluish wolf
Nearby wolf

Severe wolf

Spiralled smoke   Plucked cigars   Abundant butts
                         American leaves
Victorious vertigos   Rough alcohol   Sticky bars
                         Noachian echoes
Half-open valves   Penetrated ducts   Excited posteriors
                         Erotic machines

                         In the brown night
                         under the moonlight
                         a drunk darts about
                         in the smoke
                         of silk stockings
                         of stills
                         of wooden pipes

Winter awakening   Invigorating snows   Major refusal
                         Sudden decision

Danubian peasant   Incredible return   Elegant contact
Pétroleuse smoke
Pedestrian walk   Protective nails   Menacing tanks
Plumbous smoke
Looming towers   Cracking roadworks   Vanished arches
Irritating fumes

Here and there
gets stuck gets stuck
here and there
will get stuck
the last cab
the last rat
the last what?

Uncivil destinies   Frozen prospects   Misty futures
Historic smoke

Unsettled summer   Snuffling summer   Sweaty summer
                          Mobile summer
Long autumn   Weary autumn   Slow autumn
                          Fragile autumn
Granite winter   Metallic winter   Frozen winter
                          Immobile winter

                          The moon
                          here snows
                          on the rooftops
                          Down there
                          a star sings
                          in a very quiet
                          Pythagorean voice

Muddy spring   Chalky spring   Clayey spring
                          Mobile winter

Exotic reading   Exoteric book   Eccentric distances
                        Urban journeys
Boatman barn   Turning beaver   Bacchic brook
                        Urban journeys
Astrological battery   Masonic mansions   Alchemical dwellings
                        Urban journeys

                        Rushing through the streets
                        sometimes kings
                        appear suddenly
                        unknown magi
                        whose roving and resolve
                        the weary passer-by
                        fails to decipher

Vanished tramways   Departed coaches   Forest paths
                        Historic journeys

Twisted cycles   Sketched circles   Outlined rings
                   Civil times
Closed lines   Sealed drawings   Curved drafts
                   Uncertain dates
Soft calendars   Felt hours   False almanacs
                   Fragile futures

The comet passes
through the Lion's claws
the Dog Star howls
after the Fish
Sirius does his rounds
with the Scorpion
who twitches his tail

City smoke   Intelligent dust   Civilised mists
                   Forgotten sky

Turning heliotropes   Intertropical borage   Sweet-smelling flowers
                           Temperate land
Ardent prayer   Solar leap   Envisaged zenith
                           Lycian wisdom
Hermetic Egypt   Platonic Greece   Conquered Athens
                           Dressed-up truth

                           You mustn't
                           change barbaric
                           names
                           terms carried
                           on the backs of mules
                           on the backs of camels
                           rare words

Vegetable sun   Animal crystals   Mineral thinkers
                           Universal man

Restive mule   Fluttering butterfly   Englazed fly
                        Changing destinies
Precocious midges   Piercing lightning   Travelled pollen
                        Uncertain destinies
Bitter coaldust   Impulsive volcanoes   Convulsive rocks
                        Hesitant destinies

                        The erratic blocks
                        strewn across the plain
                        are sighing sighing
                        severed from the chain
                        A scampering mouse
                        his troubles on his back
                        doesn't know where he's going

Changing winds   Uncertain clouds   Hesitant torrents
                        Cloudy tomorrows

Icy love   Shiny breastplate   Stiffened collar
                   Fixed memories
Polished love   Cold blazon   Smooth mirror
                   Lost memory
Melted love   Dried-up pond   Weighed-down suns
                   Ancient dust

                   What are these marks?
                   A slug's trail?
                   A cuckoo's arc?
                   The cry of an owl?
                   What are these marks?
                   Down there on the square
                   the void is everywhere

Icy love   Fixed memories   Lost memory
                   Ancient dust

Rural ringdove	Autumnal ringdove	Uncertain ringdove
	Deep valley	
Wild dove	Hibernal dove	Pasty dove
	Deep alley	
Masculine lead	Soldierly lead	Nuremberger lead
	Deep oubliettes	

On the balcony
the fairy has come
to rest who
flies as high
as the seed
as the seed
far from the château

| Infantile wormwords | Puerile ana | Subtle games |
| | Uncertain childhood | |

Crinite star   Secular marvel   Remarkable curiosity
                            Costly wines
Astral hair   Prodigious century   Mysterious signs
                            Excited ducks
Dirty snow   Hydrated ball   Organic coaldust
                            Ordinary object

                            The moon settles
                            in the well
                            With a noise
                            a pebble
                            shatters it
                            Outside the sky
                            remains lit

Smoked glasses   Crashing cymbals   Celestial mechanics
                            Real childhood

Tracing shadows	Tiresome rains	Fallen snows
	Latent sap	
Forbidden networks	Numbed vessels	Dejected branches
	Underlying leaves	
Restrained leaps	Suspended gestures	Desiccated corn
	Dormant sap	

So goes the march
of short
days
So goes the frost
So goes the snow
So go the heavy
bears

Belated light	Pensive mist	Pulverulent skies
	Turning seasons	

Clever weather-vane	Magnetic needle	Agile mercury
	Distant steeples	
Atrabilious moon	Deluded clouds	Arduous roads
	Uncertain tidemarks	
Polar sign	Glistening she-bears	Boreal nights
	Serpentine journeys	

The cart
shuffles along slowly
and sometimes slips back
Like the child
who runs in a circle
Everyone finds a place
that he makes

| Certain goal | Distant goal | Extinguished imminence |
| | Serpentine journeys | |

Multiple rainfall   Shady shadows   Trampled plonk
                         Rolling sands
Habitual streams   Ragged clouds   Impure gait
                         Single-hued hippocamps
Pestilential tics   Disappearing customs Faded gestures
                         Everyday potholes

The alarm's ringing
liberates man
from morning's weight
Still sleeps the night
the day takes shape
but the mud bites
and who puts up with that?

Opaque windows   Unbreakable doors   Weeping walls
                        Luminescent eye

Infantile waltzes   Argentine bourrées   Cartesian circuits
                           Punctured circles
Saint Tropez polkas   Parisian dances   Crystalline spires
                           Muffled stamping
National festivals   Subural dancefloors   Venetian lamps
                           Clumsy twirls

                           A round cavalier
                           dances on his head
                           The ovoid seed
                           rolls right to the bottom
                           of the funnel
                           The spring writes
                           its mirror

Punctured moons   Muffled echoes   Clumsy returns
                           Boa constrictors

Clandestine wheels   Hidden drawers   Walking machines
                           Performing chaffinches
Favourable futures   Unstable futures   Faltering fortunes
                           Hidden futures
Uncertain calculations   Distant chatterings   Inoperative tables
                           Scattered questions

                           Nostradamus
                           on his great horses
                           gallops through
                           the ages the ages
                           In our time
                           cumbersome robots
                           stand about

Sacred tripod   Smoking laurels   Transparent water
                           Enigmatic worms

Customary seasons   Fraternal nights   Dazzling days
                     Listed sun
Streaming rains   Touching warmth   Shattered mornings
                     Turning moon
Gashed trees   Ploughed fields   Grass-strewn prairies
                     Rotated ground

                     During Sundays
                     the weeks slowly
                     fade away
                     During the weeks
                     Sundays grow
                     dim erased
                     by difference

Opened ground   Cut buds   Swaying grasses
                     Shooting stars

Unoccupied master   Unusual slave   Muzzled occupations
                       Parasitic explorers
Uncertain labour   Infant labour   Limping occupations
                       Eccentric inquest
Oafish inventors   Sinister right hands   Improvised tools
                       Infertile journeys

                       The eagle knows how to fly
                       the dolphin how to swim
                       man how to botch things up
                       The sun pursues
                       its impassive course
                       regardless of the planes
                       high up in the skies

Unpublished fables   Limpid proverbs   Blue-tinted truisms
                       Infallible beavers

Things born	Things faded	Things reborn
	Rebellious spring	
Everyday nothings	Transitory nothings	Transient nothings
	Unreal spring	
Airborne seeds	Erasing winds	Effaced traces
	Potential spring	

Neither late nor early
but punctual the cry
of watery sap
Where neither
high nor low
will that impatient sap
grow

Poetic labour	Botanical labour	Cosmographic labour
	Fraternal seasons	

Frozen torrents	Slow-motion Niagaras	Frozen cascades
	Damp feet	
Mellifluous rivers	Latent rivulets	Blocked streams
	Immersed fords	
Gentle brooks	Sleepy lakes	Frozen waves
	Old-fashioned dips	

From aeon to aeon
the cosmic soup
never throws up
the platonic echo
of probable knowledge
but the cinema
plays this down

| Neptunian horses | Soaring horses | Plastic horses |
| | Clear destinies | |

Worn-out rags

Hoarse concepts

Eroded soils

Mental tatters
Thumbed pages
Fought-over scraps
Browned pages
Crude currencies
Faded pages

Threadbare thoughts

Verbal rags

Crumbling words

Rust rusts
the key of keys
Vanities
will have sullied
the verses coined
in the past
where all becomes confused

Mental rags

Verbal tatters
Thumbed pages

Crumbling words

II

The collector stumbles in the marshes. These are marshes of sharp rocks and slippery pebbles. He risks spraining an ankle. Or both of them. He risks splitting his soles, slashing open the shoes' lining, tearing the uppers. Where's the water in all this, the marsh water? Sucked back to the clouds, it stares down on the uncertain track. He might just as well be spreadeagled on the ground; he finds himself like this now and then, nose done in, sometimes bleeding, with dogtooth eyes. He needs to get a grip. The sun hasn't come to a standstill for nothing, and the nights are cold, while his goal is still a distant mirage. Sometimes the rocks seem less hard, the pebbles less shifty. A few drops of rain may even fall. But no, nothing of the sort. The journey starts up again, as tough as ever. He must dig his heels in. That's life. And even beyond.

The pyramids are sleeping. That's what they do. Their form attracts sleep like a magnet, and their apex collects dreams that eat away at the heart of the innermost rocks. Amidst the convergent triangles, persistent dreams condense into parallelepiped rectangles as solid as bridges. Everything has been packed into a dense mass, unmoveable, padlocked. That's why the pyramids can sleep so quietly. When they awaken the passer-by knows nothing about it, he doesn't notice a thing. The wind stirs a little sand.

Why do these lines keep shifting? They're marked clearly on his palm, and seem indelible. The child takes an interest in stamps, plants, pebbles. As one curve becomes more pronounced, another fades. He's top of the class, he's bottom of the class. This is a child who's only just been born, who's just starting to find his feet. He's sent off to war. Events become confused. So many things seem to be going on in these illiterate jottings. And what a surprise to see new furrows open up. Even the white hairs find their echo here. Nothing but mysteries, you might well say. Nothing but mysteries.

The thick plumes of cloud have blotted out the advertisement for fine weather. We were so looking forward to clear skies, and flowers that would perfectly reflect them in their corollas. But nothing can destroy the narrow band where the stars will later appear, not even the persistent din of a machine. Rags alone move here, their flight dispersing into pure absence. The fresh grass would have shaken off the dew, the creatures would be basking in the siesta's calm, a man wouldn't bother to embrace meteorology with an elliptical and benevolent glance. But it wasn't like that. Today the skies are slate-grey: not much to write home about.

Light applause and a few whistles collided in front of the red curtain. The actor removed his mask to examine his face. He saw nothing, and couldn't deny that it was indeed the interval. The mirror, though, reflected only a walking computer. It had a cheap silver coating, otherwise it would have reflected the puppet's strings. The actor knew his part better for the following scene. It's just a parenthesis; the masterpiece has only just begun; aficionados, however, appreciate for the time being the curtain which rises up from the orchestra.

The little tree senses that its trunk is sodden. Yet the winter, while wet, has not yet awoken the sap, and the little tree is still asleep, though not in the same way as the pyramids. To each their due. Whoever has observed the snow piling up along the pavements, and seen the hail batter newly built walkways to no purpose, has one eye on the lookout for changes in the weather, however insignificant they might seem. The other eye watches the indeterminate network of ducts and sapwood. Not being short-sighted, it goes right down to the roots. People placed it there not so that it could study subterranean waters and metal cables, but through simple urbanity, careless urbanity. The little tree watches the subterranean waters flow, and the metal cables weaken. Then it forgets these considerations. It shakes itself, dries itself, pulls itself together. Someone touches its bark tentatively, with love. The little tree will spring into life.

On a ramble through the suburbs, he thinks he'll find the winning numbers. Straight and pointed, hunchbacked – or even with a double hump – thin or potbellied, monocyclist, closed, twice-circled, nines or noughts, they presage a brighter future. Tormented, the flâneur confuses numbers and codes. He has eyes only for the rhymes of the pavement, the secrets of the asphalt (memorable dates that nobody notices), the gutters perhaps methodically laid out, the diverse disgorgings and excretions. If he lifted up his nose, he would see arithmetical certainties beyond the clouds, but it is only at night time that he plunges into the vertigo of the stars. When the wheel has turned, the scraps wouldn't even be enough for a rag patchwork. That is why, without visible melancholy, he stumbles and comes to rest by the heap where he must warm himself during a winter that will last several seasons. He will end up understanding the law of quadratic reciprocity and its multiple demonstrations.

The sunflower has stopped praying in the distant room; it just turns red with embarrassment when the infant hunter asks it to. Around it are faded smiles, vague jokes in knotted bundles, scraps of fabric, odd buttons carefully collected in cardboard boxes, out-of-date atlases, almanacs, ABCs. It mucks in with the little electronic appliance, with generic products, with elementary glass. Through the window you see only myopic walls. In all that, there is a mistake at the core, an acerbic error. The sunflower has stopped praying because it never started. In reality it comes from the Auvergne, all covered in lichen and urine. The heliotrope is found elsewhere.

The travellers lost their way at the crossroads. Behind them a spectacular mountain rose up. In the distance danced the crescent moon. The scene made a beautiful setting for an allegorical morality play, simple to explain to all comers. But what theatre would put it on? Given the majestic scenery, they'd have difficulty mounting such a spectacle, and the lost travellers would find themselves once more at the crossroads, playing walk-on parts. And then, they were stumbling along faster and faster, calling out spineless instructions. They didn't even notice a group of spectators, come from God *knows* where, who looked at them without applauding or crying. They had the serious faces of children from long ago, confronted with a difficult mathematical problem. One wondered about their original destination.

The history of a day doesn't retrace the mere turning of the earth, otherwise why all these little scribblings? The cardinal points frame the four faces of the horizon and hold in their rigid angles the day and the night as well as the storm and the flat calm. Stamp your foot and you will hear the unequivocal steadfastness of the strata of the plain and the mountain. There's nothing remotely circular about the vibrations. The quadrature of the ground laying out its evidence, there would be no need for all these little scribblings to retrace the history of a day, if there wasn't something a little spherical in the air.

The cap wasn't lost, it got stuck up his sleeve. The cat didn't go astray, it was sleeping under the bed. The book will be found, the key will turn up again, the knife was lying in the hay, and the letter was on its way all the time: the sense is no longer the same. The reader thought he understood, and turned the pages with pleasure; then he began to act strangely, he started writing crookedly, he no longer knew where he'd put his hat, couldn't find the cat, picked up the wrong book, rummaged around in boxes full of keys none of which was the right one, ran about looking for his knife, and sorted empty mail. He needed to start again from the beginning. Then it turns out that the book was saying something different, that the key opened other doors, that little hiding places did not lead to big discoveries. When the horses have bolted in every direction, it takes time to round them up. Then it dawns on the reader that there was only one of them.

The hammer strikes out sparks while the horse awaits its moment. A sleigh pulls up in front of the castle full of stories, and the horse waits at the door. A distant parent arrives to pour the wine of truth, and the horse awaits its oats. The way back is circular and the sparks fly from the hammer; weary of visitors, the castle sleeps; once more, someone will drink the wine of fellowship. You first catch sight of the village from behind the crupper, tail held aloft for the fertile manure. The scorched grasses go up in smoke, turning grey just as impeccable braids do. The wolf puts its seal on the finished text, the lion watches the sun, the dog awaits its time. The moment of the horse comes and goes.

Here come the loaded horizons. Lancers appear on the level of the far off golden corn fields. This is war. The horses will gouge their track on the plain. The harvest will be lighter. The clouds roll all of this up into a blackboard and with a puff the master rubs out all of this chalk, the warriors, the mounts, the pikes. A new equation appears on the slate; now a ship sails towards a run-down port. It fires cannon balls into the water. Greek fire dances on the waves. The smoke envelops everything and it's the blackboard once more, ready for a new formula. We'll start again with the lightning, the thunder, the storms. You only have to keep your calm to find the solution.

The alarm of banners, the crush of destriers, the engulphing flames, gonfalons on halberds, the imperiosity of unions, the cross on the lance, mountains in the age of monstrous nematodes, oriflammes and pikes, the rattle of stirrups, tents unfurling, here are battles that chant, that dance, flog, gallop, hack, ignite, jump, leap, misfire, nash, overpower, prick, quarrel, reel, snort and tear with the vehemence of the great clashes recorded in literature. At the point where history tears, snorts, reels, quarrels, pricks, overpowers, nashes, misfires, leaps, jumps, ignites, hacks, gallops, flogs, dances and chants, there the destriers of the ancient warlords kick out at the pages marked with the battalion's insignia, pages dirtied in the corners by fingerprints. Electricity itself never dies, as the feeble light at the extremities of the bulb pales. The ink settles in thin reservoirs, but the victories ring out across the centuries bringing with them an equivalent weight in defeats. The wind dropped, then stopped. Somebody rolls up the fabric. It is a question of pure knowledge.

The grinding of the centuries creates a sort of powder which is very effective against doctrines. The centuries are left as unchangeable as before, while the doctrines are quickly dispersed into lagoons. Whoever goes for a walk around the lagoons will notice bloodstains fermented by marked exam papers, errata, repentances, insertions, marked doublets, delators, while orators hold forth, all ears closed. Further off, a vessel glides on the high seas. On the other side a cart goes by, slowly. In the sky, clouds pass like empires. Some clouds burst into a thousand raindrops lashing against the still surface of the water; others begin to fray at the edges: a masterpiece of baroque art, the experts say. And yet, this all fades, and centuries and centuries remain embedded somewhere in a grain of sand.

Earth: we'll begin at the bottom. The ground sinks sometimes but always covers the abyss with its absent colour. To see it in its pure state, this earth, you need to study its indeterminate richness for what it is, without satin or lace.

Mountain: neither pride nor accident, it stands by itself. It adds a new dimension to the impassive horizons, it demands an increase in respiration, it requires the head to be lifted up to better comprehend the dazzling accessories while it hides in its core the nucleus of its immensity.

Forest: it extends further than you would imagine and tracks rich in humus seem to lose themselves there. A whole network without issue rests there amongst the multiplying trunks, but the methods for describing them make the expert infallible. Squirrels move about in three dimensions like birds. Their habitat does likewise, it builds its nest and spreads its wings.

Still waters: the mirror of the sixth species does not break up the advancing clouds, but the beating feathers sketch furrows there without dreams of immortality. They disappear as quickly as ripples in water. Here are dreams which have no desire to aspire.

Flowing waters: a pure seeming makes you believe that all is in motion. The blade of straw has floated past the last bend and yet the river flows on. A ripple seems to disappear into the bank then is straight-away reborn, identical. The whole world pushes and shoves and nothing budges. Nothing budges.

Sky: at last.

III

You can turn your tongue inside out seven times, you'll still have no voice. You can choose jet black ink, the page will still be white. You can sharpen the stylet as much as you like, the signs of disease will remain invisible. You can choose colours and brushes with infinite care, the canvas will forever remain blank. Then, contradicting all you imagine, the word comes to you and it is once more possible to write. Leaves appear at the branches' ends, flowers open their corollas, fruit begins to form, nursing its seeds to maturity. The apple tree drops its apples, and the writing case supplies the fertile pen with a steady supply of cartridges.

Everything got going the instant the sun rose. The mare tugs the cart, the ox accepts the yoke, the cock plays his set from the beginning. On the white page, only a single dot was visible, while the green multiplied its images. Listening out for a unique precedent, the stone no longer awaits the paper and the scissors. We have already begun the inventory of everything. The geometrist considers the whole empty, and from this deduces the series of integers. Irrational and transcendent numbers will come to nourish the unaccountable weft. The grammarian discovers the passive conjugation. The child – it's a girl – creates a fairy with smooth, plastic, polychromatic wax.

The idea of the poem lies in the cloud. Below, the poet who thought he knew how to breathe, notices his bronchioles are a little tight. He coughs. What a cough! Everything stems from this. He goes red with embarrassment; the blood circulates a little more rapidly. The thoracic thunder rocks the foggy air. Now there are words printed on the white page. Is it the beginning of a collection? In this case, it will have to contain ten thousand things. As yet it's only a project.

He thinks he has sorted himself out, but his mind cannot escape that presence. The mistake is always there, the innumerable brood and the childhood which seemed to have melted away into far off corners wishing still to stamp and cry, in the centre of the rose field. He seemed to have found his feet, but now he's reduced to nothing but worry and chaos. Ignorance takes over once again with petulant gestures. The evidence is everywhere, on the walls, beneath the roofs, inside boxes, out of the notches. No point complaining about the number of stains. A lucid eye will silence the stammering: so long as it doesn't hang about.

Wait in the arbour, wait in the bogs, wait in the canals, wait in the deserts, wait in the elms, wait in the fields, wait in the gorse, wait in the hamlets, wait in the islands, wait in the jungles, wait in the kiosks, wait in the leaves, wait in the meadows, wait in the nettles, wait in the oceans, wait in the plantations, wait in the rocks, wait in the swamps, wait in the trees, wait in the valleys, wait in the wastes, wait in the xysts, wait in the yews, wait in the ziggurats, that's keeping an eye on a frog while biting an apple, a glass of vintage wine on the table. To act otherwise would spell danger.

Thorn bushes grow round the swamp. Scarecrows from the neighbouring fields come and nose around the place. They rummage in the mud pulling out pieces of hard rock that they throw back in and which sink once more with a splash. They lose their hats and their straw, the carnival turns nasty, absurd. They wheel about all over the place, floundering in this tatty theatre. The miserable spectacle attracts the birds from the sky. They gather to watch as the scarecrows sink beneath the mud. They will not alight on this ill-starred spot, and once more take flight.

You mustn't take fright if you descend the interminable staircase which leads from the artificial spring to the unknown winter. The steepness exaggerates its obliquity, while at times too the route levels out and you find yourself swept into a vast crowd at a virtual standstill. In time this thick and sticky juice will slowly begin to flow. Yet it leaves no trace except scraps of paper and bits of rubbery dough. When all is out in the open and the smoking chimneys are silenced, and the air is still, then the disgruntled souls panic for good reason. Those who have no fear of these sunken places, will be liberated from every human entanglement – and even others – by a ray of light.

The travellers pulled up a little after Troyes, ever unable to reach their destination. They drew nearer to it at each moment, the distance became smaller and smaller, you might even say the journey was as good as over, and yet, there was always one more step that stood between them and their goal. Yet this didn't stop them picnicking by the river. They ate their sandwiches, they clinked glasses, they picked up the crumbs, and washed their feet. Then, in high spirits, they set off once more on the road to elsewhere, their true goal, having, by way of consolation, clocked up a few extra miles on the way.

Getting out of the moving vehicle, looking backwards, the young man –
it's inevitable – ends up flat out on the hard pavement. Music will play as
his head spins in the gutter, while the engine goes on spinning in the
other sense. A few notes will later sound out on a rusted cymbal. The
result is not brilliant, he should have waited until the vehicle had
stopped. A little more patience and the left hand will play the chords
correctly, without any great skill to be sure, but all the same… The wind
whistles tunelessly on the elastic asphalt. He doesn't even have to take
shelter. The incident was all over so quickly that nobody even noticed it.
People give up sometimes for no good reason: he only needed to be
looking forwards for his little trick to have come off without upset.

At dawn everything begins with the right foot walking. Then the stars damp down their fanfares and know to stay in their places. The moon pales, then dissolves into the swamp, to turn up again beyond the night. A good poke at once strengthens and softens up the incertitude. When it reaches the end of its course, the sun darts off with elastic tread over the carpet of peat and moss. There's nothing left but to divide up the terrain into perfect polyhedrons. The old ones rebuild the lost fire in the hearth. The children sleep. The owl hoots. By the time the last candle goes out, each actor has played his part. A little patience, please, a little patience, at dawn everything begins with the right foot walking.

The zinnias are thriving, the yuccas are coming along, the wedelias are thriving, the violets are coming along, the ulmaria is thriving, the tulips are coming along, the sheep's bit is thriving, the ranunculus is coming along, the peonies are thriving, the oxeyes are coming along, the narcissi are thriving, the marguerites are coming along, the lilies are thriving, the kennedyas are coming along, the jasmine is thriving, the irises are coming along, the hydrangeas are thriving, the geraniums are coming along, the fuchsias are thriving, the eglantines are coming along, the dahlias are thriving, the corn poppies are coming along, the begonias are thriving, the anemonies are coming along. Their flowers have not yet been lopped off, the gardener's hands are not yet covered in blood. The picking season will come later. For the moment, it is forbidden to walk on the flowerbeds.

Those dried out specimens stuck between two pieces of blotting paper haven't the slightest whiff of decadence about them. A child cut off their stems for his emerald green box, and now he gives them a liturgical name. You can still hear singing in the Ciceronian style, but already the malicious man of the cloth starts babbling in the Carolingian manner, he is perhaps more crafty than he realises. The dried-out exercise book is put in a drawer with a lot of old junk. Some people prefer the change when autumn arrives. Everything bows down and shrinks. Small things take on huge importance. And then one day a zinnia comes into flower or an anemone bursts open.

Oak concurs with truffle hound, clear and distinct, in this blackish landscape. It is said that troglodytes used to press their hands against the heart of the rocks; ever since the nomads overran their homes, the cultivation of lichen has ceased. A bumblebee slips into the corolla, sticking its chest out. The musicians tune their instruments; dumbfounded, the deaf watch the harpist blowing into his instrument, while the clarinettist tightens his strings. A sharp rap of the baton alerts all ears to the now perfectly in tune orchestra. There's one of them, though, who obstinately persists in looking for cockroaches in the lion's skin, and for vipers at the bottom of the hold. In reward for his efforts, as a last grace, he will hear, when all is said and done, the gentle music of the orthoptera, and the ophidian elegy.

The return rings out from the village steeples. The din is accompanied by a bugle. Man and beast alike make their way to the top of the mountain, where camphor, butter, benzoin and incense are piled up together. From a sky cleared of every useless ingredient, lightning descends to strike the pile, which bursts into flame. Everyone receives their share of the light, the ox who pulled his cart, the caparisoned horse, the hare, the sheep, the tiger. The charcoal burners have their hands cleaned, the millers their flour sifted, the poor their clothing mended. The fire climbs right up into the sky, without eddy or smoke. The mountain rests, calm and satisfied. Man and beast come and go freely before the benevolent light.

Not a single arm goes up when the difficult question is posed. Those who could answer it hold back; their hands remain clasped on the desk, or lying flat, barely moving. Everyone tends their own garden, that's all part of practical work. Some would like to grow baobab trees, cedars and banyans, or even spurge, orchids, pittosporum. Those who sneer at 'A' grades won't even touch a violet, it might arouse suspicions. The caretaker has mislaid the keys, the headmaster can't find his set either, and nobody will help them in their search. You've already got enough on your hands following up your own enquiry.

Amongst all these little heads, there is one big one who knows what the Ptolemaic dynasty was. A fact which arouses not the slightest jealousy on the part of his peers, as the descendants of the Ptolemys don't feature on the curriculum. In reserve he also has an answer to a question on Apollonius of Perga, and another, less sure, on one about the Tian Shan. Nobody knows about this, it is simply a matter of personal pride. Little by little the sand buries the sphinx; strangers, or even some natural phenomenon, a thunderbolt perhaps, breaks open the pyramid. And yet, the significance of this dynasty shouldn't be exaggerated. It will be just as important to master coalitions, the construction of the hexagon, verb phrases. You tend your own garden, and with luck you reach your ultimate goal.

At the flea market an amateur collector finds two objects that seem to rhyme. What should he do? He goes from one stallholder to the other, haggling over the price, in a way that is quite common here. He quickly adapts to the part, but soon exhausts himself rushing back and forth, worried above all that another collector might notice the secret assonance between these two items in otherwise distinct collections. But there is no such individual. The consonance is only apparent to the eyes of one man. He tries to prop up his opinion with the support of the other senses: he fingers, he sniffs, he listens, he tastes. He asks himself if the rhyme is a full-rhyme or a half-rhyme, masculine or feminine. He doesn't rule out holorhyme. In this case the two objects make a pair and could be passed off as identical, an abstraction given what Leibniz says about the two leaves on a tree, a scientific tree, to be sure. One by one the stalls begin to close, and the onlookers move off in groups. The amateur finds himself joining one of them, abandoning the two objects to their grime, to their inertia, to their perhaps uncertain rhyme.

Meteorology didn't predict this storm which descended much to the astonishment of the experts. Mount Viso was torn from its base and propelled into the atmosphere. Why this peak should be so affected rather than another escaped the aerodynamics experts, as it did the austere geologists. Nor could anything explain the abnormal presence in the clouds of an object of such huge dimensions and of such a rocky nature, scattering fragments over the countries it happened to pass, which became embedded in the fields of wheat, oats, barley, and maize, under the name of menhirs. Though some of the astonished locals also began to refer to these great rocks as megaliths. There was disagreement, too, about the precise nature of these events. A situation which couldn't be put up with for long; one possible explanation of the phenomenon (among many others) was soon put forward. The mountain took up its place once again. The pre- and protohistorians got to work; they are still at it.

From the top of the watchtower, the madman studies the movements of the passers-by. He watches how they walk, their mannerisms, their gestures. One of them scratches himself rapidly, another coughs his guts up and spits onto the pavement, a third limps a little, just to amuse himself, a fourth, a fifth … there are so many that the madman doesn't bother to count them. He makes no distinction between women and children, nor between cats and dogs. Everything gives him equal satisfaction: he's happy to observe a general movement that concerns the whole body, or simply to note one that involves a single part. Like this, he brings his work to perfection, making apparent that which passes unnoticed, making simple appearances (like the slight tinkling of a bell) disappear.

Everyone thinks himself invisible, but that's just foolishness. Nothing should stop the eye from picking out the traces of vanished footprints, the outline of a posture, or a slowing down or quickening of the step. Who would think twice about the twitching of a little finger or the piece of peel that a more or less skilled foot has kicked aside? And yet, behind carelessly cleaned windows or indecent moucharabies, they are itemising the mannerisms, the winks, the stifled sneezes. All of these things might form the basis of an instructive discipline. Only emperors can take the air without annotation. The wind gently caresses the vegetable hair and the animal foliage. Then he takes the air in perfect peace of mind and one observes a body stripped of all irregular jolts and improbable twitchings. The picture departs a little from the idea of the project, but the intention remains clear and distinct, confident in its discrete obliquity.

The acetylene purrs away creating a stink. The stall holders set out their stands on the square that until a moment ago was decorated only by a news-stand and a pissoir. The trees don't count in the décor; they could disappear into thin air and the crowd wouldn't notice, the crowd that rushes headlong towards the coming evening when the unmade-up clowns will have finished erecting their tents. The children are dragged to a puppet theatre ruled by a skeleton dictator, who dances a jig and throws his arms and legs about, only for them to gather together once again in childish terror. In the nearby cliff ancient shells replace the more or less emaciated jesters, but science requires that we pay greater attention, it requires a fragment of jawbone. It is paramount not to mistake an innocent pebble for a maxilla. Rock hard, it survives. Even when it rests behind glass. It has given up eating a long long time ago, but there's the rub! getting two seasoned intellects to agree. The greenhorns will follow.

The servant obstinately persists in putting the tea towels with the serviettes. You might as well mix up termites and ants like some arts graduate. Books were piled up all over the house (the cleaning lady hadn't even opened the small treatise on entomology); you found them on the steps of the staircase, in the cellar, in the laundry, in the living room, on the cistern, even on the henhouse roof. One of the children put his shoulder to the task. To begin with he set to rights the authors whose first names began with the letter A. No matter if they're lame, one-eyed, or have a stammer; he set their writings apart. The others he divided up according to feast days, into three hundred and sixty-seven categories, taking account of leap years and uncertain or unknown dates. It might be that one or other of the categories remains empty; in this case a space is left for a possible future work. In the meantime, if wished, the shelf can be decorated with a bouquet of violets or a glass bowl.

The actor would do better to remain calm, but he wants the applause of the crowd whatever the cost. Little by little the cheers suffocate him, and the praise eats him up. Very little of him is left. He has nothing better to do than to watch a sugar lump in water, which dissolves like a castle in the clouds, decays like a body in the earth, is eaten up like brimstone in the fire. A quick movement of the teaspoon creates a little swirl. Then he must take his medicine. Those who have gone to watch other shows don't stop to dwell on past glories. At the top of the mountain, though, a ray of sunlight strikes a piece of quartz. Eyes turn towards him to discover that something solid is still there.

The secretaries tapped away on their typewriters, the brokers took the motorway, pacifists distributed leaflets, while agitators sent others to press with perfect calm. At the airports, the flying machines got ready to cross the seas and in the stations the bosses awaited the daily express train. The news came out as usual stuffed with consoling horoscopes. All the lightning conductors pointed to the heavens; yet nobody bothered to earth them. The thunderbolt rose up from levelled ground towards the sky. It lit up everything, then shot off, leaving behind it entire nations with their mouths agape. Nobody realised that the show would be performed again later, a floor lower down. Some scenery was quickly erected, the actors rehearsed their roles, some gesturing with their fingers, others running all over the place with great skill. The usherettes were already holding their programmes in their hands. The curtain was about to be raised for a new show.

The tragic actor knows his role by heart. He can even recite it backwards, word by word, or letter by letter. He can replace each word with a synonym or with its definition or with the eighth of its kind in this or that dictionary, glossary or lexicon. He translates it into different kinds of slang, he says it with a Normandy accent or with a Burgundy accent, he puts on a stammer, he talks through his nose, he declaims, he whispers. He follows exactly the instructions of the director who, at this level, works within reasonable limits. He will never be asked to recite his text upside-down suspended from a swinging trapeze. No, it is with two feet on the ground that the actor knows his text by heart.

Neither the fat man nor the giant are able to get inside the pillbox. They wait outside the door. And when it starts to rain, bombs or hailstones, there they remain, totally exposed. They do an about-turn, then make a dash for the squad car, which is already jam packed, somehow managing to squeeze themselves in. After less than a league, the car breaks down. Bombs or hailstones continue to fall in bucketfuls. The only option is to open the umbrella and sit down on a bench (if there is one) waiting for it to stop. The fat man hasn't forgotten to bring along a few sausages and a large round loaf to keep up his strength; the giant watches the tips of his toes getting further away, for he is still growing. Fate decides that it should stop. The sky brightens. Peace is signed. Now the fat man finds he can survive periods of prolonged frost, the giant that he can hold his centre of gravity in a respectable manner: he doesn't outstrip the summit of the highest mountain any more than his companion's circumference outstrips the mileage of the equator.

Licking the spray covered rocks, the sea gorged itself on chalk and granite; opening its mouth wide, it swallowed the contents of many water bottles and mess tins. The atmosphere purified itself with verdant branches. The fire grew fat with oil and grease, and the earth swallowed up the rubbish that had been dumped there. That's how they fed themselves, compensating for the daily decline with these feats of absorption. The quintessence played no part in these feasts. This is what amateur cosmologists think about when they go into a restaurant. Looking for the rare vintage on the opened-out dihedron, they never forget the power of waters. Perceiving the finest aromas, they never forget the power of tornados. Appreciating the hotness of the dishes, they never forget the power of flames. Leaving the bones and the left-over sauce on their plates, they never forget the power of the earth's crust. The meal is named the Big Banquet and they talk about androgyny.

From time to time a huge bubble escapes from the swamp, bursting as it reaches the surface. Might it, therefore, be possible to breathe beneath swampy ground? What creatures eke out a living in the mire without being sucked down, their lungs full of mountain air? And yet, the weight of the peat accumulates on the trade winds. They constrain it, they crush it, they hunt it. One by one the lighter creatures take flight. The remaining mass becomes volatile and begins to burn up. It turns into a black hole that neither the painter nor the traveller would notice. The light waves would turn back on themselves to travel again the paths they have already taken without leaving the slightest trace. You look at the familiar grass beneath your feet, in the distance the broad horizon. Between the two the heavy mire sometimes bubbles. The inhabitants of these parts have their suspicions; it would be wise to have a word with them.

On thin paper, in the right-hand corner, sits a man that one might describe as partly bald, partly bearded. We don't know when he was born; perhaps in another century. He is looking at or isn't looking at the waterfall. The little river winds gently along then suddenly finds itself face to face with the chasm. It leaps in with abandon, freed from the confines of the riverbed, and crashes against the rocks. The cascade turns luminescent when the sun appears. Everyone comes across it in the course of a walk; you can see it from above, leaning from the little foot-bridge, for example, or from below, being careful to avoid the splashes. Everyone bustles about to get a good look. The man in the right-hand corner hasn't moved. For him, the more the river returns to its gentle windings as if nothing had happened, the more the waterfall reveals its everlasting splendour. Here we detect the impermeability of his support: this thin paper.

The woodcutter weighs oaks, the calendar years, the tract hatred, the boxer teeth, the locksmith bolts, the confectioner sweets that melt in the mouth, the jeweller chalcedony, the circus-trainer elephants, the hairdresser combs, the hatter turbans, the tambourine maker freaks, the riding master white stallions, the juggler solid balls, the fortune teller empty balls. The weight of things demands attention, even if one cares little about the alleged law of falling bodies, for in the end everything comes to link up again: the years in the annual rings of the oak, the expression of hatred in the teeth, sweets that melt in the mouth in keyholes, precious stones in the costumes of elephants, combs behind ribbons, freaks on galloping horses, and balls as planets in topological bouquets. Now everything is clear.

This is the question: is Dominique the husband of Camille, or the wife? They announce their engagement, but without making it clear. If you don't know the family well, you wonder how you should phrase the letter of congratulations, and what present to choose. Later, they give birth to a child, Stéphane. How do you know! Do you send a doll or a suit of armour? Of course, at that age a dummy will do, which solves the problem. But others soon arise. Problems don't just occur in grammar and at the registry office. You are shown two points on a plane and asked to join them with a straight line. The sagacious Crusoe will first of all establish that the surface is Euclidian and then, with the aid of nothing but common sense, answer the question. The girl is called Dominique, and the boy Camille. Isn't there a French constable called Anne? After that, he only has to leave his desert island to rejoin polite society.

Every day at seven o'clock, it is always seven o'clock. Sometimes it's the daytime, sometimes night: always it is seven o'clock. Wars bring changes to the inscriptions on the clock faces and on the watches, but at seven o'clock it is always seven o'clock. Square clock faces come to replace round ones; looking at them closely, at seven o'clock, it is always seven o'clock. Lightning strikes the church tower, the tempest carries off the hands, the bells fall silent, the clouds hide the stars, at seven o'clock it will nonetheless still be seven o'clock. Sand appears inexhaustible, constantly flowing with the seconds, imperturbable like the years, measuring out the centuries if need be with its impeccable dance. It never rests. It carries on during sleep. If necessary, it chimes: every day at seven o'clock, it is always seven o'clock.

Obscure women hand out medals to introverted soldiers. After this anachronism, they withdrew on tiptoe to put up their barricades further afield. They spread pâté on sliced bread, they emptied gallons of red wine. They advanced beyond the perfect village. Until the enemy appeared. They exchanged fire, quadrisecting space. After this show of courtesy, the troop piled into covered trucks and headed South. The civilians were cheering the courageous latecomers as they passed. Burning oil drums lined the horizon. From time to time they stopped to spread pâté and pour out the wine. But as the invader now surrounded them on all sides, they cut their breaks short. Even the highest mountains have a fixed summit; every retreat has its end. The conquered washed their feet in the cool river, waiting, not without impatience, for someone to bring them food.

The swimmer has crossed the river of strife. He finds himself surrounded by tall grasses; soon the sun will render him dry and presentable. Over there, the nearby town clings to the sides of a hill crowned with a first rate Romanesque church. In the time it takes to sketch a picture of the terrain, the traveller has already found a place to stay, not far from the chevet, in a sort of barn where onions are drying, where dust germinates, where cats shit. Minor inconveniences for one who has reached the heart of the plains of debt: now it is from here that he must start out again. Pilgrims come to pray in the liturgical precinct for the locks to be broken down and for the chains to be cast off. He wanders off into the country-side juggling numbers all greater than zero, preferably whole numbers. Sometimes, when he stops to rest beneath the shade of a tall tree, a couplet comes into his mind, even more rich in content than in form. There's something to be positive about, it seems.

Alone, the acacias marked time. Poking through in the first days of snow, they burst forth with the coming of the rains. Nobody imagined how they would thrive when the sap began to flow once more. For all that, they didn't hold back, but, ignoring two coordinates, thrust upwards towards a third. The birds of the air came to build their nests there, and the branches multiplied until they could no longer be enumerated by the wretched accountants. Roofs watched the leaves sweeping their gutters, while in far-away fields the trees' shade made for perfect quietude. To return to the present, the fine weather completes the picture.

The foot-race champion took the wrong track; leaving the stadium, he follows roads whose names he doesn't know, crosses the suburbs, charges across fields, until he reaches the forest. The paths become indistinct, luxurious humus grows soft underfoot, but where on earth is the way out? As he goes along, the athlete scratches the bark with his nail, but he is surrounded by so many identical signs that he can't tell which marks are his own. The darkness becomes more and more insistent and when, after hours shining in vain, the sun at last goes to rest far from the ken of human eyes, his legs are left flailing about in the night. Will the runner's perseverance be rewarded? On the benches of the pododrome, spectators armed with rugs and sandwiches confidently await the bright hum of the projectors.

The twins put on weight and the sisters, who are not twins, grow bigger. Later on their personalities begin to split, and there they are, a quartet. Their spontaneous song doesn't want for harmony. They make an excursion to the forest, a forest where there are neither wolves nor satyrs, a forest that little girls can visit in safety. They come across a clearing and sit down to take a rest before going to gather some dry wood to light a fire. Not without difficulty. Yet by following precise instructions, they succeed at last. The flames rise up mixed with smoke. The air, calm until now, changes temper. The wind gets up, stirring the surrounding branches. The girls wonder if it isn't going to turn into a hurricane. Perhaps it's better to go back home. The quartet knows when to reveal its dual nature. Soon, the two sisters will get married.

The brothers scarcely resemble each other. One of them is well over five foot ten, the other is barely more than five foot. On this head grows blond hair, on that one brown, while one of them has blue eyes and the other green. Their characters are quite different too, as are their tastes, their inclinations. The one who loves the mountains sees nothing of interest in the oceans, the one who loves sailing is not drawn to the leaping goat. So, they're off, each towards a different pole, on their arduous journeys. Geography teaches us that both are covered with ice. Coming back down the slopes, you arrive once again at this slight promontory which the constant sun marks with its claw. They shake hands and remark that they still share the same name. Happy at meeting up again, they soon turn their backs on each other once more, but from now on they won't forget to send each other postcards.

Left to themselves, the Portuguese get stuck in the sand; a number of them start loading themselves up with pearls of such dubious quality that they make the almanac's compilers laugh. As for the readers, they lap up with varying degrees of satisfaction the march of the white sticks and the clowns crowned with funnels and tin pans. Outside the competitions, they stack up the tasteless wine whose bouquet has long since evaporated. Children are advised not to put their hands in fire. Also not advised, is bathing in frozen water. Having described at great length the spires beloved of tourists, the team discovers at the bottom of a crater, a lake that is perfectly smooth, perfectly clear, perfectly blue. Aesthetics forbids one from disturbing the surface, the clinic awaits those who risk this blasphemy.

Just after you've got about half way up, it's not at all uncommon to fall into a snare. The forest has an innocent look, but in fact it's booby-trapped. Anyone who thinks he can safely step off the path at this point to feel the softness of dead leaves under his feet will soon lose his way. The forester has planted major difficulties, combined rare tricks, challenged counter-stratagems, multiplied deceptive turnings. The abundance of marked paths does nothing to diminish the problem. No matter how much you try to master them, they only submit to the man who marked them out. You can lose hours here and miss the trip to the additional sights. Prudent walkers always make sure they carry some all-purpose mercerised thread in their toilet bag. Those who carry nothing end up finding their way out all the same, but at what cost...

The water in the pan soon goes cold again if you extinguish the little bluish crown that has been constructed with so much trouble by molecules of sulphur and phosphorus. Sitting before the peeling pine table, the housewife works out what remains of her savings with the stub of a pencil. She grows daily thinner thinking about the long winter days that will bring more hours of darkness, more freezing temperatures to ward off. Traffic is scarce on the snow-covered roads. The writer, hunched over the vellum of a work of aleatory literature, hesitates between two solutions: euphemism or understatement. Time passes in this kind of research. Dinner time comes round. The soup will lose its steaming perfection if the family doesn't hurry to the table. The writer, hunched over the vellum of a work of aleatory literature, carries on regardless: euphemism or understatement? It's then that he's summoned fiercely by his abbreviated first-name.

For his birthday they took him to see a fabulous light opera. Coming out of the theatre, the whole family launched into the chorus of one of the show's best songs. It was terrific. What's surprising is that afterwards the father expresses amazement over his son's altimetrical development. Yet by constantly repeating *he was born on the other side of the mountains*, you might have expected as much. Every three months they go to the tailor: the child is becoming expensive. The father kicked himself for suggesting this outing in the first place; from now on they would manage things differently. And yet, his trousers continued to get too short three weeks after they'd been made. Fortunately, they got all their squandered money back when the fairground set up its stalls in the square. The organ grinders who knew many another old chorus, were able to use the seat of his pants for strings.

The hunter returns from the forest, the fisherman from the river, the labourer from the fields, the housewife from market, the ferryman from the other bank, the jockey from the racecourse, the policeman from his beat, the chemist from his laboratory, the marksman from the firing range, the architect from the building site, the undertaker from the cemetery. The man who has returned from nowhere makes marks on various materials, in which the undertaker recognises the deceased, the architect the house, the marksman his target, the chemist his mortar, the policeman his truncheon, the jockey the horse, the ferryman his barge, the housewife meat, fruit and vegetables, the labourer the plough, the fisherman fish, the hunter game. Everyone comes to a standstill in front of such a work.

Unless it's a stag, one sees the head of the animal straight on. The eyes may be positioned on the sides, you won't find the enigma any less arresting. If it's a praying mantis, a fulgorid or even a housefly, the difficulty turns out to be considerable, if only in the formulation of the equation. As for solving the problem, this sometimes turns out to be impossible. The point of intersection might be at infinity. More frequently, though, to a far from negligible extent, half-hinted at words are exchanged through eye-contact. With a little goodwill, if the face is human, there will be some effect, eventually. This depends on dangers nearby, or distant, shoulder-to-shoulder harassment or imminently disseminating panic. Or else the wind carries off briefings and projects, or else passing right over their heads lets things take their own course. Above every coat of arms, the sky remains impassive.

A monotonous chant could be heard issuing from the dome: if a wave of nostalgia came over him, he would count the days on his fingers and the calculation took so long that sleep overcame him as if he'd been counting sheep, of which there were certainly plenty in the nearby mountains. The night passed so quickly that scarcely had the chant ceased than an urgent sound of brass filled the air, dawn hardly broken. Along with the rush arrived many young plants that came to join already mature specimens. A few shouts and the lot was laid out neatly in staggered rows. Everybody was now pressed together shoulder to shoulder. If a word happens to escape, there exist methods for bringing it back to its proper usage. It will find its place again in the foyer of memory.

The crop produces the new bouquets. Is the gardener moving forward? That's the question which the rushed visitors don't ask. They look at the flowers with uninquisitive eyes, unconcerned about their roots or the quality of the seed. And then, wouldn't they be utterly astonished if one put this question to them: is the gardener moving forward? Perhaps they would think that the question made no sense because of the onion that the gardener always carries about in his waistcoat pocket, an old-fashioned accessory that is perhaps out of step with fashion. It's no longer astonishment that fills them, though, but incredulity, even stupefaction, if they discover that the gardener is not moving forward, but that he is rising. His foot on his spade, elbows tucked in, his head resting on his hands, there he is in effect floating high above the flowerbeds, the flower baskets and the neat borders. This slight levitation could well cause a great deal of bother for the humble labourer if a visitor were to catch sight of him. Fortunately, nobody notices this slender displacement, a staggering feat for the man who performs it, and who asks himself many, many questions, as he confidently surveys his prize-winning seedlings.

The big zebra was far too noisy. He outstripped all his companions in height, and by the quality of his stripes, but above all it was the power of his neighing that singled him out. As for racing, he wouldn't even try it, knowing too well that amongst his companions there were quite a few that were far quicker than him. They were wary of his kick, which was quite capable of being used unexpectedly to take them out. Some albinos, who had wished to form a splinter group, were forced to rejoin the mob by their fellows, for he had shown an alarming sympathy for their cause. Abandoning the flat, customary in solidungulate races, he leapt about on the green hills astonishing the farmers, at least those who wished to be astonished. Then he turned to singing. He shut himself away in distant caves to develop his repertoire. This retreat didn't last long at all, for he had no lack of confidence in his skill. He wanted to test his gifts in front of the zebras who grazed over the river. When he appeared, the false note he gave out caused a riot. The fabulist in residence got his ears boxed.

There's a small group of them who sit themselves down every day on the brim of the well, a well so deep that you wonder who could have dug it out in the first place; perhaps it's a natural phenomenon? In any case, you can't reach the bottom, which makes it practically useless, as even with miles and miles of string, the bucket still wouldn't reach the surface of the liquid. If indeed such a surface exists. Nobody knows. There's a small group of them who sit themselves down every day on the brim of the well and sometimes, out of the blue, one of them thinks he has hit upon a way of reaching the water. He explains his crazy plan; the others laugh. Sadly, they move off. He might get replaced by somebody else. Or not; but things always end with the arrival of a newcomer who, letting himself be seduced, sits himself down on the brim of the well, and waits.

Research is being carried out into the four seasons that disappeared so long ago. Specialist organisations are looking into the question; they are bent over the problem; they release hypotheses; they envisage solutions that they can never substantiate. In fact, everyone knows very well what the problem is, but nobody wants to see the truth unmasked, yes, everyone knows the key to the mystery: the four seasons are playing leap-frog with communal living-space. And then, almanacs can be seen flowering in the January sunshine, bringing their hypotheses, their problems, their questions, with the answers in the back for those with a low IQ. At the edge of the swamps swollen by the recent rains, amateurs exhaust themselves running in a square; then the dust storms come and the mire turns into powder, so that they give up their pointless circuit-training. Their faces alter or their eyes brighten, but little understanding what has really taken place.

Deep in the woods, shadows sing the virtues of cabbage soup. Their subtle voices fail to penetrate the ears of the pétanque players and the bare-breasted prostitutes. Such types, too taken up with their everyday pursuits, will never wake up to the simple charms of a brisk family walk. The voices carry on nonetheless, gently bouncing from tree to tree, unconcerned with bad weather, independent of historical change. A more just view of things, more correct, rectifying even, and prescriptive, puts the human species in its place, however sympathetic it is. Besides, it is not in the least despicable, to give this knowledge its full weight, to learn that cabbage soup is made in a pot.

The elder brother has become the chief of the tribe. They take essential tools with them and plunge into the forest, making for a destination they already know. An inner knowledge resides within them, they have inherited behaviour patterns for the occasion. Their column passes between thick grown trees, pushing its way through dense ferns, to emerge on spongy moss. No need of little white pebbles, for the way back will be found just as easily. The tribe make a short stop for a bite to eat, then once more set off towards the castle where they are expected. They will marry the ogre's seven daughters, who will give birth to lots of children, all very rich.

The clock has stopped on the edge of the track. It couldn't tick away indefinitely without finding somewhere to rest. To this end, it has chosen the edge of a wood. A felled tree provides a seat. A few mushrooms grow around the still standing stump. The woodcutters must be sleeping nearby, axe stuck in the bark, saw resting on the moss. There are other parts to the horometer: this cord made of vegetable matter, this heavy weight, these little cogs whose raw materials had to be searched out in distant lands. For the moment everything is at rest, awaiting the benevolent railway worker who will set things in motion again, while the woodcutters wake up to make new incisions.

In the apartment, there's a room given over to junk. The grandmother used to sleep there in times gone by. She's still alive, the grandmother, but she no longer stands in the way of her son-in-law's storage concerns. The daughter stacks up old newspapers in the deserted room (for the grandmother has voluntarily chosen to live elsewhere). The window has a far from cheerful prospect, overlooking the courtyard. The old newspapers are joined by dusters, ribbons, lace, scattered remnants of cloth, and the child's school books. He doesn't have a brother, so they only get used once. Much later, the adolescent will hit on the idea of selling them. For the time being, he's stuck in bottom set for geometry and algebra. One day in summer, he looks at last year's textbook and, suddenly, amidst the solitude of abandoned objects, he understands. A million insights lead him rapidly to integral calculus; but this isn't the right way to proceed. A little more method is required. You need to nurture new theories, feeding them with exercises, bathing them in verification, washing away any errors. Then the wind of certainty will blow at the summit of acquired knowledge.

Geology brings the children to the promenade. This presents a certain danger, for the Kimmeridgian cliff easily crumbles. Two amateur geologists suffered long and agonising hours here when they were trapped by a landslide in the last century. Caution is imperative therefore, and the hammer should be wielded with the utmost care. Then creatures flake away from the chalky rock that lived in times more distant still than that of the two amateurs, and who were willing to die in the appropriate manner to live on in a mineral state. They calcified, and now they come to light again, only to vanish once more, in general. Afterwards, they are found in drawers; the happiest amongst them have the right to the feeble daylight afforded by dusty glass cases. The children don't waste time over these nostalgic considerations, they scatter joyfully among the rocks. Is it really true that these creatures lived millions of years ago? One might wonder. Natural history has only just been born.

Before it was domesticated, lightning performed miracles. It came in via the chimney, greeted those present, made its way to the dresser, smashed a plate or two, passed under the table, circumnavigating a few soles, then departed at last through the closed window without so much as disturbing a fold in the curtains. Sometimes, more viciously, it smashed into a bell tower which burst into flames; all the townspeople rushed along to talk about it, bringing with them so many buckets that, besides, were of little use. Later on the church was rebuilt. Rare and coloured materials were mixed together to achieve a roughly equivalent effect. People likewise gather together to mark pyrotechnic displays with their cries of wonder; the fireworks over, the crowd remains standing an instant where it is, but this time there is nothing to rebuild.

When the fair has finished, the visitor moves off with his memories. He sifts through them as he climbs the long incline which leads to the bridge over the river; after that, he only has a few crumbs left, which he keeps for the next stage of the journey. In the smoke-filled cabaret, he shares news of the neighbouring country with the locals; people listen to him incredulously, without ever shrugging their shoulders. In no way does he try to impress them. He passes on his way, leaving scarcely a trace, a little suspect to stay. The dust of long miles has accumulated on his boots, many dogs have barked at his heels, many villages have vanished behind his back. In the current state of affairs, he can't be tracked down. What he carries off, nobody knows, for nobody can predict the sifting of his memory.

The morning rain didn't stop the pilgrim. With good reason, for afterwards the wind came to turn a greyish sky green. Then the emerald colours turned to azure. The wind continued to blow strongly on the stretched-out plateau. The pilgrim made no attempt to struggle, he let himself be carried like a dead leaf. His steps became strides, his strides long gliding itineraries. He was swept from the ground only to find his feet again a little, or a lot, further on, landing sometimes softly, sometimes with a bump. Will he reach the gates of the walled town like this? Specialists operated the drawbridge. In his sack he carried scale models of the five Platonic solids and the thirteen books of a famous work. Otherwise how to get in?

The six sides of a cube mark out a cross on the ground. With the addition of a circle the game begins. After eighteen years of stagnation, everybody is fed up with cubes, spheres and astragals. They start to experiment again with hopping, throwing a disc into the air. Some people suggest variants; sometimes one finds hell, an altar, a table, or a moon at the centre of the cycle of days. Nobody is obliged to make use of these, and the first version is currently the most common, by far; but the pleasure is unanimous when, the sun buffeted by clouds, rains crash down, shifting the ancient disc with great splurges of mud. And it's a real swamp that the children end up splashing about in.

One false note and the pigeons fly off in all directions. Hovering around on the lookout for scattered crumbs, they were hastily gobbling up these charitable morsels, when the noise that disrupted their customary pleasures occurred, with a miry grating followed by a kind of sonorous explosion somewhere between a boom and a vroom. The worn-out machine did nothing more. Blind to this fact, and judging things simply by what they heard, the pigeons scattered into rectilinear, but disparate, flight paths. Fallen debris from the group was found on the edges of roofs, on the branches of the trees, and on the arms of the statues. Several feathers fall back down to earth, pointless witnesses to a scattering already described.

The water that he is watching refuses to boil. Not even a single bubble detaches itself from the bottom of the pan to rise to the surface and burst. At most, you could say that the waters are stirring, but it doesn't develop into a storm. With an abrupt turn the impatient man hurries into the sitting room to look at the time. When he comes back, the water is dancing happily with huge bubbles, all steaming with joy, bursting with goodness. Now he only has to use it. It is best not to try this with milk; it has no conception of the static ballet, it knows only how to run off in vast waves, leaving nothing behind but a yellowish silt. If you carry on regardless, all turns black with rage. The law is tough, but it's the law; if you change it you may right an injustice, but you usher in disorder.

The area isn't entirely built-up, there are still some gardens and a few fields. There may be a stiff breeze, the earthworms will scarcely be aware of it, tucked away in their underground passages. How not feel sympathy for these obscure workers? They feed the soil with their fertile work and ask for nothing in return. They live modestly, self-assured, sincere. And yet the bipeds on the surface haven't a good word to say about them; they never stroke them as they deserve. In the days when animals used to talk, open discussions took place between the oligochaetes and man. In our day, in his metropolitan homes, man no longer contributes to the improvement of the soil. The other continues his artisan's work.

The giraffe has put its hoof on the stepladder to reach the lowest leaves of a tree with a bare trunk. The sun casts little shadows on its larger than life neck, while it struggles on the last step. A fully extendable ladder would have been much better, but where on earth would you find one in a country full of groundnut and white bears? The old roadmender would be glad to offer his advice, but his voice is so cracked that the sound of it couldn't reach the ears of the perched animal. The giraffe climbs back down from its pedestal, pleased enough with its harvest. It knows just when it's in danger of going too far.

The captain marks his position. He measures angles, he calculates, he records in his logbook numbers that the articulate dolphin knows by heart. The latter will soon have completed his work as escort and, while a friend of men, will move off towards the open sea when the port displays its cranes on the horizon. The ship's cook prepares the last meals. The ship advances with good speed, leaving its wake behind. Tomorrow, perhaps, they will check their bearings. On the still far-away quays of the maritime port, firemen practise to avert a possible disaster. A light and unobtrusive rain scatters as a precaution; it will not extinguish the fire in the revolving beam of the lighthouse, which has been protected against all such mixtures.

At eleven fifty-nine as at twenty-three fifty-nine, the end is approaching. The little hand moves cautiously towards the final seconds; every time, it makes the same gestures. Yet the instrument contains no chiming bells and everything will take place in silence. Sliding with certainty over the frozen ice rink of time, the big hand reaches its goal. Yet it doesn't stop there, but continues in its course, providing that, and only providing that, the clockmaker has put the mechanism back together properly. One can then consider, with satisfaction, the round accomplished. To get there, it would have been necessary to move heaven and earth.